gifted

DISCOVERING AND CULTIVATING YOUR SPIRITUAL GIFTS

Lifeway Press®
Brentwood, Tennessee

ISBN 978-1-4300-8359-7
Item 005845747
Dewey Decimal Classification Number: 248

Subject Heading: RELIGION / Christian Living / Spiritual Growth

Printed in the United States of America

Student Ministry Publishing
Lifeway Resources
200 Powell Place, Suite 100
Brentwood, TN 37027

We believe that the Bible has God for its author; salvation for its end; and truth, without any mixture of error, for its matter and that all Scripture is totally true and trustworthy. To review Lifeway's doctrinal guideline, please visit www.lifeway.com/doctrinalguideline.

PUBLISHING TEAM

Ben Trueblood
Director, Student Ministry

April-Lyn Caouette
Production Editor

Karen Daniel
Manager, Small Group Resources

Shiloh Stufflebeam
Graphic Designer

Kyle Wiltshire
Writer

TABLE OF CONTENTS

INTRO

When I hear the word "gifted," I usually think of two things. The first is from my childhood. When I was a kid, there was a program at my school for the "gifted" students. Only the brightest students, the ones who had shown the most ability and potential to excel academically, got to be in the program. I always wanted to be in that program!

The second is from my teenage years, when I discovered the X-Men comics and cartoons. The X-Men are humans who have "mutant" abilities. A man named Professor Xavier finds them as children and teenagers and brings them together at a school for "gifted youngsters." There, they become a team and learn how to use their amazing abilities to fight evil and defend the world.

Many Christians take one or both of these perspectives on giftedness into the church. They mistakenly think that the only believers who are "gifted" are those with the most personality, ability, or intelligence or that only certain believers have gifts. This couldn't be further from the truth. Every believer is gifted!

This book will help you learn about your giftedness. You will learn about the God who has given you these gifts, what they are, what they are for, why they are important, and how you can use them. If you've placed your faith in Jesus as Lord, you are gifted. Keep reading to learn more.

ABOUT LIFEWAY STUDENTS

Only God and His Word bring about true heart transformation. Because of this, it is our top priority to ensure our resources are rooted in the truth of Scripture. Our desire is to create trustworthy resources that help fuel ministry.

Gifted: Discovering and Cultivating Your Spiritual Gifts was written by Kyle Wiltshire. Kyle is a writer and editor with Lifeway Students, and he lives with his wife, Joni, and three children, Noah, Micah, and Lilly, in Hendersonville, Tennessee.

HOW TO USE THIS BOOK

This book includes five sessions, each covering an important aspect of spiritual gifts. Each session explores Scripture that will help students answer essential questions about spiritual gifts.

GROUP TIME

Each session starts with a section called "Let's Begin." Here you'll find questions and illustrations to help begin discussion. There are also Icebreaker options for each session in the Group Guide at the back of the book.

The rest of each session will explore key questions and aspects of spiritual gifts and how they impact the lives of students.

KEEP GOING

There are four days of devotions at the end of each session to help students continue to learn and grow.

GROUP GUIDE

Both individuals and groups can use this book to learn about spiritual gifts. See page 66 for tips on leading this study with a group.

WHO IS THE HOLY SPIRIT?

God is three Persons in one. We call this aspect of God "the Trinity," and it's one of the most amazing mysteries of the Christian faith. One of the three Persons of the Trinity is the Holy Spirit, and in this chapter, we will explore who the Holy Spirit is and how He works in your life. You cannot understand spiritual gifts without understanding who the Holy Spirit is.

group time

LET'S BEGIN

Have you ever visited a museum? It's possible you hear the word "museum" and the first thing you think is "BO-RING!" Sometimes that can be true, but not always. Recently my family and I visited Washington D. C. and went to the National Archives. While we were there, we saw copies of the Declaration of Independence, the Constitution, and the Bill of Rights. It was quite amazing to see these items that are so important to our country with my own eyes! They are so old that it's hard to see the ink on the paper.

Maybe you've visited a museum you thought was cool, or maybe you've seen some ancient artifacts at some point. It's pretty amazing to see a piece of history.

What is the oldest thing you have ever seen? Where did you see it?

Do you find it interesting to see things that are very old? Why or why not?

Think about this: everything we've ever seen on earth had a start date, no matter how new or old it is. That means that at some point, it didn't exist. There is only One who is eternal, only One who has no start date.

THE ONE WITH NO BEGINNING

You've probably already guessed it, but God is the only One who has no beginning or end. He has always been—no one created God. In fact, the opposite is true. It is God who created everyone and everything else.

In the beginning God created the heavens and the earth. Now the earth was formless and empty, darkness covered the surface of the watery depths, and the Spirit of God was hovering over the surface of the waters.

What are three interesting things you find in these verses?

1.

2.

3.

Here we see that not only did God create the heavens (the universe) and the earth, but His Spirit was also there, hovering over the surface of what He had just created. In fact, in Colossians 1:16-17, we learn that Jesus was present at creation as well. This means all three Persons of the Trinity were there, active and involved at the beginning of everything.

Why is it important that God the Father, God the Son (Jesus), and God the Holy Spirit all worked together in the creation of the world and everything that exists?

This is important because it reveals the unity found within God. There is no division. There is not one Person of the Trinity who is greater than the other. God—all three Persons—created the world and everything in it. This is helpful to know because it informs our understanding of who the Holy Spirit is as we learn more about Him.

THE ROLE OF THE HOLY SPIRIT

Even though all three Persons of the Trinity are totally unified, they have different roles. This means they accomplish different tasks and work in different ways. The work of the Holy Spirit is different from the work of the Father and different from the work of the Son.

Read John 16:7-15.

> "Nevertheless, I am telling you the truth. It is for your benefit that I go away, because if I don't go away the Counselor will not come to you. If I go, I will send him to you. When he comes, he will convict the world about sin, righteousness, and judgment: About sin, because they do not believe in me; about righteousness, because I am going to the Father and you will no longer see me; and about judgment, because the ruler of this world has been judged.
>
> "I still have many things to tell you, but you can't bear them now. When the Spirit of truth comes, he will guide you into all the truth. For he will not speak on his own, but he will speak whatever he hears. He will also declare to you what is to come. He will glorify me, because he will take from what is mine and declare it to you. Everything the Father has is mine. This is why I told you that he takes from what is mine and will declare it to you."

In these verses, Jesus is speaking to His disciples. It was just hours before He would be betrayed, falsely accused, crucified, and killed. He wanted to help the disciples know that even though He was going away, Someone else would come and be with them. They would not be alone.

According to these verses, what are three different things the Holy Spirit does?

1.

2.

3.

This explanation of the roles of the Holy Spirit doesn't reveal everything He does, but it helps us know some of the basics. Let's highlight three important elements of the work of the Holy Spirit.

THE HOLY SPIRIT IS OUR COUNSELOR

A *counselor* is someone who advises you and helps you know what to do in certain situations.

> Who has been a good counselor to you? What makes someone a good counselor?

The Holy Spirit wants us to make good choices. He helps us know what we should do, which direction to take, and how to live in a way that shows others we belong to God. The Spirit's counsel is always for His glory and our good: when we do what He says, God is shown to be awesome, and we are helped too.

THE HOLY SPIRIT CONVICTS

To *convict* means to declare that someone is guilty of an offense. In a spiritual sense, when the Holy Spirit convicts us, it means that we know inside that we've done something wrong.

> What does it feel like when the Holy Spirit convicts you?

To feel conviction from the Holy Spirit might be painful, but ultimately it's a good thing. It's His way of helping us to turn away from what we've done wrong, to seek God's forgiveness, and to end the cycle of returning to that same sin again and again.

The Holy Spirit also convicts those who aren't believers, empowering them to turn their hearts from their sin through repentance and to place their faith in Jesus, receiving new life and purpose.

THE HOLY SPIRIT GUIDES IN TRUTH

If we only listened to ourselves and let our feelings guide us to what we think is true, we would never find what is actually true. We would always bend the "truth" to fit what we want and what we think is best for us. This means there is no such thing as "your truth" or "my truth" when it comes to God's Word. His truth doesn't change, no matter how we feel about it.

> When has the Holy Spirit guided you in the truth, changing your mind from a wrongly held belief to a right one?

Thankfully, the Holy Spirit helps us know what is true. He shapes our hearts and leads us to live in truth (see John 17:17). Believing Him and following the truth He leads us to is for our good. We know this because He loves us and has proven His love in Jesus's life, death, and resurrection (see Rom. 5:8).

THE HOLY SPIRIT LIVES WITHIN US

Here's why Jesus said it was for our benefit that He was returning to heaven and not staying on earth (see John 16:7)—His leaving meant the Holy Spirit would come.

Read Acts 2:1-4.

When the day of Pentecost had arrived, they were all together in one place. Suddenly a sound like that of a violent rushing wind came from heaven, and it filled the whole house where they were staying. They saw tongues like flames of fire that separated and rested on each one of them. Then they were all filled with the Holy Spirit and began to speak in different tongues, as the Spirit enabled them.

This is the story of the arrival of the Holy Spirit on the day of Pentecost, fifty days after Jesus rose from the grave. Prior to this, the Holy Spirit didn't come to stay in the lives of believers. He would empower someone for a specific task or time, but He wouldn't remain. After Pentecost, the Spirit came to live in the hearts of believers forever.

What are some signs that the Holy Spirit lives within someone?

As we saw in Acts 2, when the Holy Spirit came upon the believers, they were empowered with gifts. In this specific instance, they were given the ability to speak in different languages. And on that day, it so happened that thousands of Jews from all over the known world had gathered in Jerusalem to observe Pentecost, all speaking different languages. Through the power of the Holy Spirit, each person heard the gospel in his or her own language (see Acts 2:6). On that day, three thousand people repented of their sins and were baptized—and the church was born.

This is the heart of this book: the Holy Spirit is the One who comes to live inside you when you place your faith in Jesus. When He does, He gives you at least one spiritual gift that can be used to glorify God and build up the church. This means that if you are a believer, you are gifted!

How does it make you feel to know that the Holy Spirit has gifted you to serve God?

CLOSE IN PRAYER.

Thank You, God, for sending Your Spirit to live within me. As You counsel, convict, and guide me into truth, help me to listen to You and obey You. As I learn about the gifts You have given me, help me to use them for Your glory and to build up Your church. Amen.

Keep going and growing in your knowledge and understanding of the Holy Spirit by completing the next four days of devotions.

Day 1 will give you the opportunity to go further into the Word of God. Today let's spend some time deepening our understanding of who the Holy Spirit is and what He wants to do in us.

But the fruit of the Spirit is love, joy, peace, patience, kindness, goodness, faithfulness, gentleness, and self-control. The law is not against such things.

The word "fruit" is singular in this passage, not plural. Why does this matter?

If we are not strong in one of these areas, we don't get to dismiss it as "not my thing." We must be growing in all nine of these areas. That is why these are the "fruit" of the Spirit, not "fruits."

Which of these qualities of the fruit of the Spirit is most difficult for you? What needs to happen in your heart to let the Spirit grow you in that area?

As the Holy Spirit grows us in these areas, our character is shaped, Jesus becomes more evident in our lives, and God is glorified. The Holy Spirit doesn't just give us gifts—He transforms us and grows us in love, joy, peace, patience, kindness, goodness, faithfulness, gentleness, and self-control.

CLOSE IN PRAYER.

Lord, help me to allow Your Spirit to grow love, joy, peace, patience, kindness, goodness, faithfulness, gentleness, and self-control in me so that I can become who You want me to be. Amen.

Psalm 119:11 says, "I have treasured your word in my heart so that I may not sin against you." Day 2 will focus on treasuring God's Word by giving you different ways to memorize Scripture.

Read 1 John 4:4.

You are from God, little children, and you have conquered them, because the one who is in you is greater than the one who is in the world.

This verse is a great reminder that the Holy Spirit who lives in you is greater than the enemy. Memorizing this verse can help you fight temptation by reminding you who the Holy Spirit is and how He can help you defeat sin.

Use the following technique to memorize 1 John 4:4. Read the verse several times. Then try to remember it with only the first letter in each word revealed as a hint.

Y__ a__ f____ G___, l_____ c_____, a__ y__ h_____
c_____ t_____, b_____ t___ o___ w___ i_ i_ y__ i_
g_____ t_____ t__ o___ w___ i_ i_ t_____ w_____. 1 John 4:4

Repeat this process until you can fill in the blanks without help. Then try it again without using the first letters as a hint.

____ ____ _____ ____, _____ _____, ___ ____
_____ _____ _____, _____ ____ ____ ___
__ __ ____ __ _____ _____ ____ ____ ____ __ __
____ _____. 1 John 4:4

Once you have the verse memorized, write it on a note card. As you memorize more verses, your stack of note cards will grow. Review them frequently. Memorizing Scripture will help you treasure God's Word in your heart.

CLOSE IN PRAYER.

Day 3 will focus on prayer—an important practice for growing your relationship with God.

Read Hebrews 4:16.

Therefore, let us approach the throne of grace with boldness, so that we may receive mercy and find grace to help us in time of need.

In this verse, the writer helps us understand that because of Jesus, we can speak freely to God and boldly approach Him with everything on our hearts. Spend the next few minutes praying, using the PRAY acronym below. Feel free to write your prayers in a journal, or just let the words, descriptions, and suggested verses below guide you as you pray silently.

PAUSE: Don't rush. Examine your heart and see if there is anything you need to confess as you begin your time of prayer. Listen for the Spirit as He prompts your heart (see Ps. 139:23-24).

REJOICE: Give praise and thanks to God for who He is and for all He has done (see Ps. 100).

ASK: Bring your requests to God, both you own needs and the needs of others (see Phil. 4:7).

YIELD: Submit yourself, your desires, and your will to God. Give Him control of your life (see Luke 22:42).

CLOSE YOUR TIME OF PRAYER.

God, I am so grateful that You allow me to come into Your presence and speak with You. Help me to listen to You and obey You. Your will be done in me. Amen.

On Day 4, you will have options. You can spend time silently reflecting on what you've learned this week, journaling, or doing something that reveals the truth of what God has taught you.

Read James 1:22-25.

But be doers of the word and not hearers only, deceiving yourselves. Because if anyone is a hearer of the word and not a doer, he is like someone looking at his own face in a mirror. For he looks at himself, goes away, and immediately forgets what kind of person he was. But the one who looks intently into the perfect law of freedom and perseveres in it, and is not a forgetful hearer but a doer who works—this person will be blessed in what he does.

REFLECT: What have you learned about the Holy Spirit this week? How can you be a doer of the Word this week, with the help of the Holy Spirit?

JOURNAL: Using a notebook or journal, write about who the Holy Spirit is. How is He counseling you, convicting you, and guiding you in truth?

GO AND DO: Have you been ignoring the Holy Spirit's prompting to do something specific? If so, don't put it off. Be obedient to Him in faith and with confidence. Otherwise, spend some time praying specifically about how you can walk closer in step with the Spirit (see Gal. 5:25).

CLOSE IN PRAYER.

Spirit, guide me. Change me. Make me more like Jesus every day. Help me not to try in my own strength to walk faithfully with You but to let You work and move through me. Amen.

WHY ARE SPIRITUAL GIFTS IMPORTANT?

In Session 1, we learned that spiritual gifts are from the Holy Spirit and that every believer has at least one. However, being from the Holy Spirit isn't the only reason why spiritual gifts are important. In fact, spiritual gifts are crucial to God's plan for the world to know Jesus.

LET'S BEGIN

Have you ever had to wear a cast? When I was in college, I broke my ankle playing basketball. I had to wear a cast for twelve weeks! When my cast was finally removed, I thought I was going to be able to jump right back onto the basketball court. I was wrong! I could barely stand on that ankle. I had to wear a walking boot for another two weeks and do physical therapy. Then I had to wear a brace for another few weeks after that. Only then could I return to the basketball court.

Having a broken ankle impacted my whole life. It affected how I walked, the clothing I could wear, how I took a shower (I couldn't get my cast wet!), and which activities I could participate in. It's amazing to think that even though I only injured one part of my body, it influenced everything else.

Have you ever had an injury that affected your whole body? If so, what was it? How did it impact you?

When I was injured, I couldn't say to my ankle, "You're just a small part of my body. Get over yourself!" Just because my ankle wasn't my brain or heart—organs I can't live without—didn't mean that the rest of my body wasn't affected. It's the same way for us as individuals within the church, the body of believers.

ONE BODY, MANY PARTS

Read Romans 12:4-5.

Now as we have many parts in one body, and all the parts do not have the same function, in the same way we who are many are one body in Christ and individually members of one another.

As believers, we are one body of faith in Jesus. He unites us in our purpose in life and in our mission as His disciples. Every believer has spiritual gifts, but none of us have exactly the same mix of spiritual gifts and qualities that make us who we are. This means each follower of Jesus is like a different part of the body. Every person has a role to play. Some roles are more public, and others are more behind the scenes. Not every person is gifted to pastor a church, but that doesn't make other gifts less important or valuable to the entire body of faith.

Think about the church you are part of. How have you seen people with different gifts serve in different ways?

As we learn more about our spiritual gifts, we'll see how the gifts God has given each of us work together to accomplish the mission of Jesus.

GOOD STEWARDS

In the film *Return of the Jedi*, Han Solo agrees to let his frenemy Lando Calrissian use his ship, the Millennium Falcon, for a crucial battle against the Empire. "I'll take good care of her," Lando assures him. "She won't get a scratch." Han Solo looks longingly at his ship. "I got your promise now. Not a scratch."[1]

In essence, Lando was agreeing to be a good steward of Han's ship.

Read 1 Peter 4:10-11.

Just as each one has received a gift, use it to serve others, as good stewards of the varied grace of God. If anyone speaks, let it be as one who speaks God's words; if anyone serves, let it be from the strength God provides, so that God may be glorified through Jesus Christ in everything. To him be the glory and the power forever and ever. Amen.

When have you agreed to be a good steward of something that belonged to someone else?

Spiritual gifts are from God. No, we don't unwrap them like birthday presents, but they are still gifts, and since they come from God and not from ourselves, we must take care of them—or steward them—well. According to 1 Peter 4:10-11, how should we take care of our spiritual gifts?

List three ways we steward our spiritual gifts well according to 1 Peter 4:10-11.

1.

2.

3.

God has given us spiritual gifts to serve others. They are not intended to be used for our own gain or fame. We can serve in many ways, but God desires for us to use the gifts He has given us for the advancement of His kingdom through the church. This doesn't mean that the only time we can use our spiritual gifts is within the four walls of a church building; it just means that we use them to serve others and for the growth of His kingdom.

We must also use them in God's strength, not our own.

How do we do something in God's strength and not our own?

Doing something in God's strength begins with our perspective. We must realize that He is the One who works through us; we're not using strength that comes from within ourselves or mustering up our own ability. We must listen for His voice and follow His guidance. This means we must be prayerful and sensitive to the Holy Spirit's leading by being in step with Him (see Gal. 5:25). We also must have a heart that's committed to doing what He wants and not what we want.

When we use our spiritual gifts to serve others and in the strength God provides, this brings glory to God.

> What are three ways you can bring glory to God in your everyday life today?
>
> 1.
>
> 2.
>
> 3.

Glorifying God means He is the One we are living to please. We aren't trying to earn His favor or our salvation, though—we want to please Him because we love Him. We use the gifts He has given us so that when something amazing happens, others say, "Wow! God is good!" rather than "Wow! You are good!"

SIX IMPORTANT TRUTHS ABOUT SPIRITUAL GIFTS

Let's put it all together now. Why are spiritual gifts important? Here are six elements that reveal the importance of spiritual gifts.

1. SPIRITUAL GIFTS HELP US UNDERSTAND GOD.

James 1:17 says that "every good and perfect gift is from above, coming down from the Father of lights, who does not change like shifting shadows." God is gracious and giving. The gifts He has given us, including spiritual gifts, are evidence of His goodness.

2. SPIRITUAL GIFTS HELP US UNDERSTAND OURSELVES.

We are greatly loved by God. This is made most clear in Jesus (see John 3:16). If we were not so deeply loved by God, He would not have given us the Holy Spirit or spiritual gifts. He has done these things because He is good and because we are precious in His sight.

3. SPIRITUAL GIFTS HELP US UNDERSTAND THE CHURCH.

In 1 Corinthians 12:12-31, the apostle Paul clearly explains that every part of the body of Christ (the church) is important. Everyone has value. Each believer receiving spiritual gifts is proof of this.

Open your Bible and read 1 Corinthians 12:18-26. What do you think Paul means in verse 22 by "weaker" parts? Why are "weaker" parts actually indispensable?

4. SPIRITUAL GIFTS EQUIP US TO FULFILL GOD'S MISSION.

In Matthew 28:18-20, Jesus gives us the mission of our lives, also known as the Great Commission. As followers of Jesus, making disciples is what our lives are supposed to be about. Spiritual gifts help us fulfill that mission. If we tried in our own strength to tell everyone in the world—using every language—that Jesus is Lord, we'd never leave our own street. Only through the power of the Holy Spirit in us, using the gifts God has given us, can the world hear the truth about Jesus.

5. SPIRITUAL GIFTS EQUIP US TO SERVE THE BODY OF CHRIST.

In 1 Corinthians 12:7, the apostle Paul says, "A manifestation of the Spirit is given to each person for the common good." This means that the gifts the Spirit has given us are designed to help us serve and encourage each other within the church. Spiritual gifts aren't just talents. They truly are special powers given to us by God to serve the church and make disciples.

6. SPIRITUAL GIFTS HELP US DISPLAY JESUS IN OUR LIVES.

You can use your spiritual gifts anywhere, not just in a church building. Through the gifts you have received, you can help others know Jesus and be a blessing to others at school, on your sports teams, playing online video games, and in all of your activities and interests.

When have you seen someone using a spiritual gift outside of a church building?

Spiritual gifts have huge importance in our lives. As you learn more about them in general, as well as what your specific gifts are, you'll grow in your understanding of their importance.

CLOSE IN PRAYER.

Thank You, God, for revealing Your deep love to me by giving me the Holy Spirit. Help me to listen to You, stay in step with You, and grow in my relationship with You. Remind me every day of the importance of the gifts You have given me, and help me to use them for Your glory. Amen

Have you ever heard the phrase, "Same but different"? It's a way to say that two things or people are both similar and unique at the same time. This is a perfect way to explain the work of the Holy Spirit in our lives.

In your own words, how would you summarize these four verses?

Read 1 Corinthians 12:4-6, 11.

Now there are different gifts, but the same Spirit. There are different ministries, but the same Lord. And there are different activities, but the same God works all of them in each person... One and the same Spirit is active in all these, distributing to each person as he wills.

There is only one Holy Spirit, and He moves and acts as He pleases (see John 3:8). The Spirit who lives in you is the exact same as the One who lives in me. However, the Spirit has given you different gifts than He has given me. God custom-fit your gifts for you, and He did the same for me.

How has God used your uniqueness in the past for His glory?

God wants each of us, with our uniquenesses and different gifts, to be led by the same Spirit to accomplish His will on earth.

CLOSE IN PRAYER.

"But you will receive power when the Holy Spirit has come on you, and you will be my witnesses in Jerusalem, in all Judea and Samaria, and to the ends of the earth."

These are the last words of Jesus recorded in the book of Acts, and they reveal some important truths. First, the Holy Spirit gives us power. Second, we are to be a witness for Jesus everywhere we go. Finally, our destination is the ends of the earth. That means God desires for every person everywhere to know who He is and come to faith in Him.

Let's memorize this important verse as a reminder of these truths.

"B___ y__ w___ r_____ p____ w____ t__ H_____ S_____ h__ c_____ o_ y___, a___ y__ w____ b_ m_ w_____ i__ J_____, i_ a___ J_____ a__ S_____, a__ t_ t___ e____ o_ t___ e_____." Acts 1:8

Repeat this process until you can fill in the blanks without help. Then try it again without using the first letters as a hint.

"
_____ _____ _____ _____ _____ _____ _____ _____ _____ _____ __ ____, ____ ____ ____ ___ ___ _____ __ _____, __ ___ _____ ____ _____, ____ __ __ _____ __ ____ _____." Acts 1:8

Once you have the verse memorized, write it on a note card. As you memorize more verses, your stack of note cards will grow. Review them frequently. Memorizing Scripture will help you treasure God's Word in your heart.

CLOSE IN PRAYER.

"Stop fighting, and know that I am God, exalted among the nations, exalted on the earth."

Some versions of the Bible translate the phrase "stop fighting" as "be still." Let's do both right now and spend some time in prayer using the ACTS method below. Don't rush this time. Be still before the Lord and stop fighting against the quiet and the lack of distractions. Allow Him to speak to you.

Feel free to write your prayers in a journal, or just let the words, descriptions, and suggested verses below guide you as you pray silently.

ADORATION: Spend a few minutes just telling God how great He is (see Ps. 8).

CONFESSION: Spend a few minutes confessing your sin before God. Ask Him to reveal anything hidden in your heart that you need to confess (see Ps. 51:1-13).

THANKSGIVING: Take inventory of your life and give thanks to God for every blessing you have (see Ps. 138).

SUPPLICATION: This means to make requests of God. Pray on behalf of others and pray for the needs in your life (see Matt. 7:7-12).

CLOSE YOUR TIME OF PRAYER.

Holy God, You are good! I confess that I fall short and need Your grace everyday. Thank You for gifting me with Your Spirit. Help me to use what You have given me for Your glory. Amen.

Spend time today silently reflecting on what you have learned this week, journaling, or doing something that reveals the truth of what God has taught you about the importance of spiritual gifts.

Read Ezekiel 36:26–27.

"'I will give you a new heart and put a new spirit within you; I will remove your heart of stone and give you a heart of flesh. I will place my Spirit within you and cause you to follow my statutes and carefully observe my ordinances.'"

REFLECT: What have you learned about the importance of the Holy Spirit this week? How can you follow God more closely, with the help of the Holy Spirit?

JOURNAL: Using a notebook or journal, write about the importance of the Holy Spirit. How is He removing your heart of stone and giving you a heart of flesh?

GO AND DO: Have you been ignoring the Holy Spirit's prompting you to do something specific? If so, don't put it off. Be obedient to Him in faith and with confidence. Otherwise, spend some time praying specifically about how you can walk closer in step with the Spirit (see Gal. 5:25).

CLOSE IN PRAYER.

Spirit, guide me. Change me. Make me more like Jesus ever day. Help me not to try in my own strength to walk faithfully with You, but to let You work and move through me. Amen.

WHAT ARE THE SPIRITUAL GIFTS?

There's a difference between talents and spiritual gifts. God can certainly use your talents for His glory and His kingdom—your potential is something He gave you when He designed you before you were born. However, not all talents are spiritual gifts. The point of spiritual gifts is to glorify God and encourage, nourish, and strengthen the body of Christ. This chapter will explore what the specific spiritual gifts are that God uses to do these things.

group time

LET'S BEGIN

I love superhero stories. Whether it's a movie, TV show, or book, I'm in! One of my favorite heroes is Spider-Man. His character has been around for decades yet remains popular and relevant today.

Who is your favorite superhero and why? If superheroes aren't your thing, what are you really into and why do you love it so much?

From the start, one of the recurring themes throughout Spider-Man's stories has been the responsibility of power. Many times throughout the Spider-Man comics and films, the character's Uncle Ben is quoted as saying "with great power comes great responsibility,"[1] a phrase that influences Spider-Man's moral compass throughout his life.

Even outside the realm of superheroes, this is a true statement. If you're in the marching band, you have great power and responsibility: if you play the wrong note or don't march in correct formation, it throws everyone else off. If you are on a sports team and you don't run the play the right way or are careless with the ball, it impacts everyone.

How have you personally experienced the responsibility of power?

Unlike fictional superpowers, spiritual gifts truly are supernatural powers given to us by God when we come to faith in Jesus. They are to be used responsibly and with great care. So what are these powerful spiritual gifts found in Scripture? This session will help you find out.

TWO TYPES OF GIFTS

Read 1 Peter 4:11.

> If anyone speaks, let it be as one who speaks God's words; if anyone serves, let it be from the strength God provides, so that God may be glorified through Jesus Christ in everything. To him be the glory and the power forever and ever. Amen.

In these verses, we find two broad categories of spiritual gifts—**serving gifts** and **speaking gifts**. This isn't an "either-or" sort of thing; a person can have both serving and speaking gifts. Also, speaking is involved in serving gifts and vice versa. Both types of gifts are used to serve God and share the gospel with others. The gifts are designed to work together to accomplish the common goal of glorifying God and building up the church.

Where else in life do you find two different things that work together to accomplish a common goal?

SERVING GIFTS

Another way to describe serving gifts is that they are "people focused." Often, people who have serving gifts are those who can make things happen.[2] The serving gifts found in the Bible are **administration, leadership, helps and service, mercy, giving, faith, healing,** and **miracles**. Let's take a moment and briefly explore each one.

Administration: The gift of administration is found in 1 Corinthians 12:28, and it describes people who can organize and mobilize others in ways that are vital for a healthy church community.[3]

Leadership: The gift of leadership is listed in Romans 12:8 and refers to people who have a vision and can both articulate that vision and lead others into the future.[4]

Godly character is required to use the gifts of administration and leadership in the way God intended (see Matt. 20:25-28). Jesus modeled these gifts in how He led His disciples.

Who do you know who exhibits godly character in how he or she organizes things or leads? How does this person show these characteristics?

Helps and Service: Every follower of Jesus is called to help and serve others, but there are some people who have specifically been given a supernatural gift of being able to help and willingly serve. This gift is often expressed in a willingness to do practical jobs that others don't want to do (see 1 Cor. 12:28; Rom. 12:7).

Mercy: As with the gift of helps and service, every Christian is called to be merciful. However, there are some who are gifted by the Holy Spirit to extend mercy exceedingly well. Those with this gift can show compassion and offer hope in a unique, God-sized way (see Rom. 12:8).

Giving: All Christians are called to give, but those with the gift of giving do so in a selfless way that's empowered by the Holy Spirit. Giving is their first instinct; and this involves more than just giving money. It includes giving time, resources, and energy as well (see Rom. 12:8).

How do the gifts of helps and service, mercy, and giving build up the body of Christ?

It's plain to see that churches could not function without people who have and use these gifts for God's glory.

Faith: Faith is the root of everything when it comes to following Jesus. However, those with the gift of faith have a supernatural trust in God that allows them to move with confidence and assurance when others might not (see Rom. 12:9).

Healing and Miracles: These two gifts are listed separately in the Bible, but we'll look at them together. It's clear that healing and miracles were vital parts of the ministry of Jesus and in the early days of the church. It is also clear that these gifts are less common today. But that doesn't mean they do not happen anymore. The bottom line is: if these gifts occur today, they are for God's glory and to serve others, not to make a show or dazzle an audience (see 1 Cor. 12:9-10).

Of the serving gifts we've just discussed, which ones have made the biggest impact on your life? How have you been impacted by them?

SPEAKING GIFTS

In his book *Spiritual Gifts: What They Are and How to Use Them*, author Dan Darling says, "Speaking the words of God is a holy calling, whether it's preaching in a large church, sharing Scripture over coffee with a brother or sister in Christ, or teaching children in Sunday School."[5] This is so important to remember when using speaking gifts. Like we've already stated, speaking gifts require service, and serving gifts require speaking. However, there is an increased weight of responsibility when telling someone, "This is what God says . . ." This is never to be done lightly or for selfish gain but to build up the church.

Apostleship: All of the apostles we read about in the Bible are with Jesus now. So the gift of apostleship today is connected to missions and a desire and supernatural ability to help the gospel spread to places where it is not, as the apostles of the early church did (see 1 Cor. 12:28; Eph. 4:11).

Evangelism: Every Christian is called to tell others about Jesus (see Matt. 28:19-20). However, for those with the gift of evangelism, it comes a little easier. These people can build relationships, process and communicate deep theological truths, and help people learn how to effectively share the gospel with others as well (see Eph. 4:11).

Prophecy: This gift has two components: foretelling and forth-telling. Yes, sometimes a person is gifted to be able to tell what will happen in the future (this is called "foretelling"). However, today prophecy is more exhibited in the ability to diagnose a situation and share the truth of God's Word with people in impactful ways that speak to their lives and circumstances ("forth-telling") (see Rom. 12:6; 1 Cor. 12:10; Eph. 4:11).

Has someone ever spoken to you in a way that helped you see the need to live differently? Who was it? What did they say?

Teaching: The gift of teaching is the ability to explain God's Word to others in such a way that they can understand it and apply it to their lives. This gift is not limited to pastors and preachers—anyone who opens God's Word with the desire to help others understand it can have this gift. In 1 Corinthians 12:8, the apostle Paul says that the Holy Spirit gives wisdom and knowledge to those with the gift of teaching to help them understand Scripture and pass it on to others (see Rom. 12:7; Eph. 4:11).

Exhortation: The gift of exhortation is a supernatural combination of the abilities to comfort, counsel, and encourage others. Everyone who follows Jesus needs to exhort others, but those with this spiritual gift are empowered by the Holy Spirit to do so even more effectively (see Rom. 12:8).

Who has taught you from the Bible or encouraged you in a way that helped you and shaped your life? How did this person do that?

Discernment: Those with the gift of discernment have the ability to know what is true and what is untrue and lovingly help others know the difference as well. In 1 Corinthians 12:10, the apostle Paul called this the ability to "distinguish between spirits." There are forces of evil that desire to deceive people. People with this gift are needed in great supply today.

Tongues/Interpretation of Tongues: There is much debate among believers about what these gifts are and how they operate in the world today. But simply put, the gift of tongues is the ability to speak in other languages, and the gift of interpretation is the ability to communicate what is said in other languages to those who hear it. The point of these gifts is the same as for all other spiritual gifts: to glorify God and strengthen the body of Christ. That is why they always go hand in hand. In a teaching or worship context, it does no good for someone to speak in another language if those listening can't understand what is being said (see 1 Cor. 12:10,28,30; 14:27).

These are the spiritual gifts found in the Bible. This list might feel a little daunting, but it's helpful to recognize these gifts for what they are designed to do—glorify God and build up the church. Anyone using a spiritual gift in any other way is misusing it. Spiritual gifts are not about the person who receives them but about the God who gives them. They are a source of great spiritual power. And with great power comes great responsibility.

CLOSE IN PRAYER.

Thank You, God, for giving me spiritual gifts. Help me to use what You have given me to glorify You and build up Your church in the process. Thank You for teaching us what spiritual gifts are through Your Word. Amen.

Read 1 Corinthians 12:27-31 in your own Bible.

These verses can be somewhat confusing. The apostle Paul makes it clear that all spiritual gifts are vital for the church and equally important. Is he changing his tune now, ranking them in importance and telling people to want the "better" gifts?

What do you think? From what you've learned about spiritual gifts to this point, do you think Paul is ranking them in importance and telling people to want only the "better" gifts? Why or why not?

It's always important to read the Bible in context. Look at what comes immediately after these verses: the famous passage about love in 1 Corinthians 13.

Read 1 Corinthians 13 in your own Bible.

Why would Paul write about love right after explaining spiritual gifts?

Considering everything Paul wrote about spiritual gifts, it wouldn't make sense for him to now throw all of that out the window and say, "These are the better gifts." Sure, having some gifts like teaching or leadership will put you in front of people, but that doesn't make them better. Paul is making it clear that no matter what your spiritual gifts are, the "even better way" is to use them with love (see 1 Cor. 13:1-3).

CLOSE IN PRAYER.

Read 1 Corinthians 13:13.

Now these three remain: faith, hope, and love—but the greatest of these is love.

Most people don't often consider that the chapter about love, 1 Corinthians 13, is sandwiched between two chapters about how to correctly think about and use spiritual gifts. What Paul is trying to get across is that love must be at the center of the gifts God has given us. You might be the most gifted person ever to live, but if using your gifts is not motivated by God and love for others, then your are just making noise!

Let's memorize this verse as a reminder that love is the greatest.

N___ t_____ t_____ r_____: f_____, h_____, a___ l_____ –
b__ t__ g_____ o__ t_____ i__ l_____. 1 Corinthians 13:13

Repeat this process until you can fill in the blanks without help. Then try it again without using the first letters as a hint.

____ _____ _____ _____: _____, _____, ____ _____–___
__ _____ __ _____ __ _____. 1 Corinthians 13:13

Once you have the verse memorized, write it on a note card. As you memorize more verses, your stack of note cards will grow. Review them frequently. Memorizing Scripture will help you treasure God's Word in your heart.

CLOSE IN PRAYER.

Lord, whatever I do, let Your love be at the center of it all. Amen.

One of the best ways to spend time in prayer is to use the prayer Jesus taught as His model prayer. This prayer, also known as "the Lord's Prayer," is not Jesus's way of saying that this is the only way to pray. It is simply a good foundation and guide for prayer.

Read Matthew 6:9b-13.

"Our Father in heaven, your name be honored as holy. Your kingdom come. Your will be done on earth as it is in heaven. Give us today our daily bread. And forgive us our debts, as we also have forgiven our debtors. And do not bring us into temptation, but deliver us from the evil one."

What are elements you see in this prayer?

Take the next few minutes to pray these words again. Go slow. Think about what you are saying. Say these things directly to God.

Then pray some of the elements you see in this prayer, like honoring God, asking for provision, forgiving others, seeking forgiveness, and asking for deliverance from temptation.

CLOSE YOUR TIME OF PRAYER.

Holy God, Your will be done in my life. You are great and I pray that You would be glorified through me and how I live my life. I ask for wisdom and understanding as I seek to use the gifts You have given me for Your kingdom and glory. Amen.

Spend time today silently reflecting on what you have learned this week, journaling, or doing something that reveals the truth of what God has taught you about the importance of spiritual gifts.

Read 1 Peter 4:10-11.

Just as each one has received a gift, use it to serve others, as good stewards of the varied grace of God. If anyone speaks, let it be as one who speaks God's words; if anyone serves, let it be from the strength God provides, so that God may be glorified through Jesus Christ in everything. To him be the glory and the power forever and ever. Amen.

REFLECT: What have you learned about this week the spiritual gifts found in Scripture? How can you speak about God and serve Him more closely with the help of the Holy Spirit?

JOURNAL: Using a notebook or journal, write about the spiritual gifts found in Scripture. How is God being glorified in your life?

GO AND DO: Have you been ignoring the Holy Spirit's prompting you to do something specific? If so, don't put it off. Be obedient to Him in faith and with confidence. Otherwise, spend some time praying specifically about how you can walk closer in step with the Spirit (see Gal. 5:25).

CLOSE IN PRAYER.

Spirit, guide me. Change me. Make me more like Jesus every day. Help me not to try in my own strength to walk faithfully with You, but to let You work and move through me. Amen.

SESSION

04

HOW DO I
LEARN WHAT MY
SPIRITUAL
GIFTS ARE?

We've now reached the place in this book where you will start learning more about what your spiritual gifts are. This book doesn't have a test or inventory to help you figure out your spiritual gifts. Instead, our desire is for you to do four things to determine what your gifts are: 1) reflect on who God has made you; 2) explore the Scriptures; 3) spend time in prayer, seeking the Lord for guidance and clarity; and 4) try things, help out, and see what fits and where God leads.

group time

LET'S BEGIN

It starts earlier and earlier each year. Decorations go up. Commercials start popping up on streaming services and TV. Stores begin preparing. You hear the music everywhere you go. Anticipation rises. You know what I'm talking about: Christmas! Everyone loves the Christmas season, but the best part is Christmas morning. There's nothing like waking up and seeing the presents under the tree, gathering with family for a great meal, making memories, and celebrating the birth of Jesus with other believers.

Think back over your whole life. What has been your favorite Christmas gift to this point? Why was it your favorite?

One of my favorite moments on a Christmas morning is when I get handed a present and I still have no idea what it is. The mystery and excitement are fun—but sometimes when I finally unwrap the present, it's a bit of a letdown.

Describe a time when an present ended up being a letdown.

As we continue our exploration of spiritual gifts, we have arrived at the point when we will seek to discover what gifts the Holy Spirit has given you. This process will most certainly not be a letdown because He knows you and has gifted you exactly as He wanted.

WHO ARE YOU?

Read Psalm 139:1-16 in your own Bible.

In this Psalm, David made two things abundantly clear—God knows us and He made us (wonderfully at that). This means none of us were made by mistake: we each have exactly the characteristics and qualities that He wants us to have. However, remember that we are also each born with a sin nature that is not from God (see Ps. 51:5). This means we can't excuse sin of any kind in our lives as "this is just how God made me." For all of us who have placed our faith in Jesus, our desire is to become more like Him and deny our sin nature through a process called *sanctification*. This means that as we grow in our relationship with Him, we are continually transformed to be more like Jesus.

> With this understanding in mind, think about how God has made you. What are you good at? What talents, skills, and abilities do you have? List at least three.

> What things are you interested in or passionate about? List at least three things.

> Ask a friend or leader in your church to answer the same two questions about you and record their responses below.

It is important for us to know that God made each of us unique. He gave us natural abilities and talents, as well as other things we've cultivated over the course

of our lives due to interests and passion. However, it's also important to know that our talents, abilities, interests, passions, and spiritual gifts aren't always the same (although they can be). Therefore, we can't automatically link these things together and say for certain that we have a spiritual gift in a certain area simply because we have a talent in that area. We also can't say we *aren't* gifted by the Spirit in an area simply because we aren't talented in
that area.

WHAT DOES THE BIBLE SAY?

If talents, abilities, interests, and passions do not always equal spiritual giftedness, how can we determine what our gifts are? This is a good place for us to remember what the Bible says about spiritual gifts.

Spiritual gifts are listed mainly in four places: Romans 12:3-8, 1 Corinthians 12, Ephesians 4:11-16, and 1 Peter 4:10-11. In all these places, the same four themes emerge:

1. Each believer was given at least one spiritual gift the moment the Holy Spirit came to live in him or her.

2. All the gifts are given to glorify God and for building up the church.

3. All the gifts are important, even though they have different functions and purposes within the church.

4. All the gifts are to be used humbly and through the power God provides, not for selfish gain.

Go to the back of this book (pages 75-76) and read over the list of gifts that we've covered. After reading the list of gifts, which ones stand out to you as possibilities for the gift(s) you have been given? Write two below along with brief summaries of what those gifts are.

1.

2.

Why do these gifts stand out to you as possibilities?

It's possible these gifts resound with you because you are good at them. For example, you might be a person who, without thinking about it, gives your coat to someone you see who needs it. This could indicate that you have the gift of giving. Or it's possible you have always been organized and able to make sense of chaos. This could mean you have been given the gift of administration.

Ask a friend or church leader if she or he has noticed something special about you that you might not have noticed about yourself. Write her or his answer below.

Here is how awesome God is: sometimes He puts a gift in someone that is completely the opposite of his or her personality. For example, some of the shyest people are also the most amazing Bible teachers. Through the gifting of the Holy Spirit, they can command the attention of a room and powerfully offer the most profound teaching. But in a relational setting, these individuals might be very reserved and quiet. This is God showing that He is the One determines our gifts; our natural abilities or personalities don't determine them.

> **Have you ever known someone who served God powerfully in a way that is the opposite of her or his personality or natural tendencies? Who is it and how has God used this person in your life?**

In 1 Corinthians 12:11, we are reminded, "One and the same Spirit is active in all these [spiritual gifts], distributing to each person as he wills." The point is, God is the giver of the gifts, and He gives as He sees fit. No one earns a gift for being more important or better than anyone else.

WHAT DO I DO NOW?

I hope that you aren't frustrated at this point if your gifts haven't been clearly revealed to you. God isn't trying to make it difficult. However, He does want to shape your heart in all things, so searching for your spiritual gifts might be a tool He wants to use to help you grow.

There are some ways you can continue to seek Him and discover your gifts. It all begins with having the right perspective. Near the end of Jesus's earthly life, after sharing with His disciples that He was going to be crucified, two of them came with a request. They asked to sit on Jesus's right and left hand side in His kingdom, the places reserved for the two most important people in a group (apart from the leader). This was the complete opposite approach to what Jesus had been teaching them and revealing to them through His own life.

Read Mark 10:43-45.

> "But it is not so among you. On the contrary, whoever wants to become great among you will be your servant, and whoever wants to be first

among you will be a slave to all. For even the Son of Man did not come to be served, but to serve, and to give his life as a ransom for many."

The path to greatness in Jesus's kingdom is through service. Start out with the desire to serve Him through your spiritual gifts and you will be starting out on the right foot.

What are ways you can serve Jesus right now in your church, school, home, or neighborhood?

The next thing you can do now is spend a lot of time in prayer. Here are three thing things you can pray for right now to help you discover your spiritual gifts:

1. **Ask God to help you know your gifts.** James 1:5 reminds us that God loves to give wisdom to those who ask Him for it. As you look for opportunities to serve, ask Him to show you how He has gifted you.

2. **Ask God to give you opportunities to try things.** Ask God for open doors of opportunity. If someone asks you to help do something with your church or in a faith community, prayerfully consider saying yes, even if it's out of your comfort zone.

3. **Listen for the Holy Spirit affirming your gifts through others.** Sometimes others see things in us that we do not yet see in ourselves. If you hear the same things over and over again about the way you're gifted, it could be the Holy Spirit speaking to you through another person.

As you close this group time, either by yourself or with a friend, pray these three prayers.

CLOSE IN PRAYER.

Holy Spirit, thank You for gifting me. Help me to discover the gifts You have given me and to use them for Your kingdom and Your glory. I want to serve You and to have the right heart. Amen.

Read 1 Corinthians 14:1-5 in your own Bible.

When you read these verses, does it seem like Paul is saying that people with the gift of prophecy are better than people with the gift of tongues? Why or why not?

Once again, these verses might be confusing. Here is a brief summary of what Paul was communicating to the church at Corinth:

- Exercising the gift of prophecy when speaking before the whole church is a good thing because it builds everyone up.

- Exercising the gift of tongues is very encouraging to the person speaking, but it isn't encouraging to the person listening unless there is someone to interpret what is being said.

- Ultimately, Paul was helping the Corinthian church to know that, as with any gift, using the gift of tongues is meant to build up the church, not to glorify the person using the gift.

What is a takeaway for you after spending some time reading and thinking about these verses?

No matter what gifts you have, use them for God's glory and to help others grow closer to Him.

CLOSE IN PRAYER.

But the fruit of the Spirit is love, joy, peace, patience, kindness, goodness, faithfulness, gentleness, and self-control. The law is not against such things.

The evidence of the Spirit's work in our lives is not that we can do amazing things with our spiritual gifts but that we are living out these nine qualities. Letting Him grow this fruit in our lives helps us stay in step with the Spirit (see Gal. 5:25). And the fruit of the Spirit can help you know how to use your spiritual gifts to the maximum glory of God and benefit of the church.

Let's memorize this verse as a reminder of the work the Spirit is doing in your life.

B__ t__ f_____ o_ t__ S_____ i_ l___, j__, p_____, p_____, k_____, g_____, f_____, g_____, a___ s_____-c_____. T__ l__ i__ n___ a_____ s_____ t_____. Galatians 5:22-23

Repeat this process until you can fill in the blanks without help. Then try it again without using the first letters as a hint.

_____ ____ _____ ___ ___ _____ ___ _____, ____, _____, _____, _____, _____, _____, _____, ____ _____-_____. ___ ___ ___ ____ _____ _____ _____. Galatians 5:22-23

Once you have these verses memorized, write them on a note card. As you memorize more verses, your stack of note cards will grow. Review them frequently. Memorizing Scripture will help you treasure God's Word in your heart.

CLOSE IN PRAYER.

Another great way to pray is to pray Scripture back to God. Use this section of Psalm 25 as a prayer. Read it out loud if possible. Don't be in a hurry. Feel free to read it as is or rephrase it in your own words.

> Make your ways known to me, Lord;
> teach me your paths.
> Guide me in your truth and teach me,
> for you are the God of my salvation;
> I wait for you all day long.
> Remember, Lord, your compassion
> and your faithful love,
> for they have existed from antiquity.
> Do not remember the sins of my youth
> or my acts of rebellion;
> in keeping with your faithful love, remember me
> because of your goodness, Lord.
> The Lord is good and upright;
> therefore he shows sinners the way.
> He leads the humble in what is right
> and teaches them his way.
> All the Lord's ways show faithful love and truth
> to those who keep his covenant and decrees.
> Lord, for the sake of your name,
> forgive my iniquity, for it is immense.
> **Psalm 25:4-11**

"Guide me in your truth and teach me." This is a great prayer to use as you seek to discover your spiritual gifts. Open your heart to be taught by the Holy Spirit and guided in the truth by Him.

CLOSE YOUR TIME OF PRAYER IN YOUR OWN WORDS.

Spend time today silently reflecting on what you have learned this week, journaling, or doing something that reveals the truth of what God has taught you about the importance of spiritual gifts.

Read Romans 12:3-8 and 1 Corinthians 12:4-11 in your own Bible.

These verses list most of the spiritual gifts that are mentioned in the Bible. Take some time to pray and focus on these verses and how the Holy Spirit may have gifted you.

REFLECT: What have you learned about the spiritual gifts found in Scripture this week?

JOURNAL: Using a notebook or journal, write about the spiritual gifts you are discovering.

GO AND DO: Have you been ignoring the Holy Spirit's prompting you to do something specific? If so, don't put it off. Be obedient to Him in faith and with confidence. Otherwise, spend some time praying specifically about how you can walk closer in step with the Spirit (see Gal. 5:25).

CLOSE IN PRAYER.

Spirit, help me know how You have gifted me. Help me accept opportunities to learn about the gifts You have given me, and help me to use them for Your kingdom. Amen.

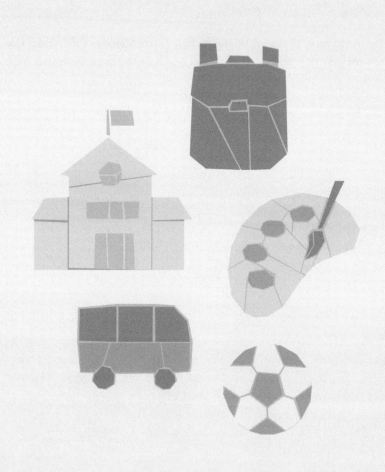

HOW DO I USE MY SPIRITUAL GIFTS?

Now is the time for the water to hit the wheel and the rubber to hit the road. The time when push comes to shove. All of these phrases mean the same thing—it's time for action! In this final session, we'll explore how we can use the spiritual gifts that God has given us.

group time

LET'S BEGIN

Many times when you buy a new product or download a new app, you can find a section in the instructions called the FAQs—Frequently Asked Questions. The people who made that product or app have realized that many of their customers have the same questions about it, and the FAQ section is an attempt to anticipate these questions and answer them. They hope to lessen confusion and help the person who wants to use the product feel more informed.

After four sessions of exploring spiritual gifts, what questions do you still have about them?

Read 1 Timothy 4:14-15.

Don't neglect the gift that is in you; it was given to you through prophecy, with the laying on of hands by the council of elders. Practice these things; be committed to them, so that your progress may be evident to all.

Paul wrote two letters to a young pastor named Timothy, whom he loved dearly and with whom he had a very close relationship. In these verses, Paul challenged Timothy not to neglect the gift he had been given and to practice using it. Our desire is that you learn how to use your spiritual gifts and to practice them. Hopefully, in this final session, we'll be able to answer some of the FAQs about spiritual gifts so that you will feel equipped to begin using them now.

What is at least one spiritual gift you believe you have? (If you are doing this study as a group, allow each person in the group to answer this question.)

TALENTS AND SPIRITUAL GIFTS

We've touched on this already, but let's spend some more time discussing how talents and spiritual gifts work together. Hopefully this will give you some ideas for how you can begin using your spiritual gifts now. Remember, talents and spiritual gifts are not always the same.

What are some talents that aren't spiritual gifts? Name three.

1.

2.

3.

Let's use sports and music, for example. The Bible doesn't list the spiritual gift of speed, hand-eye-coordination, or singing on pitch. These are talents and interests you are born with and also cultivate over years of practice and playing. They aren't spiritual gifts themselves, but they can work alongside spiritual gifts.

How can you use a talent like basketball or playing the trumpet alongside a spiritual gift?

Here is an example: Say you're an amazing soccer player. You can combine your ability to play soccer with a gift like apostleship. Seem crazy? It isn't. The gift of apostleship is the supernatural ability and desire to help the gospel get to places where it currently is not—in many places around the world, soccer is far more welcomed than the gospel. You can go places as a soccer player and build relationships, then through those relationships help people come to know Jesus. See how God can take a talent and amplify it with a spiritual gift?

Discuss a few more scenarios where talents and spiritual gifts can go hand in hand. How could a talent complement the following spiritual gifts? (Use pages 75-76 for a reminder of what the Bible lists as spiritual gifts.)

Helps and Service:

Administration:

Teaching:

WHERE CAN YOU USE SPIRITUAL GIFTS?

We've said before that spiritual gifts are meant to glorify God and build up the church. But that doesn't mean the only place we can use them are within the walls of a church building. You can use spiritual gifts at home, at school, in your neighborhood, online—anywhere.

Home:

School:

Neighborhood:

Online:

For instance, if you have the gift of teaching, you can use that to discuss God's Word at school, at a coffee shop, ina locker room, or anywhere else people gather. If you have the gift of discernment, you can use that as you play a video game online when the group chat gets off color. You can skillfully—and aided by the Holy Spirit—steer conversation away from things that are inappropriate or vulgar and back in a more positive direction. You can even find ways to plant seeds of the gospel as you play with others.

As believers, we are the church (see 1 Cor. 12:12: one body, many parts). We do not live alone and function as "lone wolves." We must be joined with other believers, inside the walls of a church building and outside of it too. When we use the gifts

God has given us to encourage, support, and love others, it brings Him glory, and it also contributes to lift up the body of Christ. Our gifts were intended to be used in community.

How can using your spiritual gifts build community?

FAN INTO FLAME

Read 2 Timothy 1:6-7.

Therefore, I remind you to rekindle the gift of God that is in you through the laying on of my hands. For God has not given us a spirit of fear, but one of power, love, and sound judgment.

In the New International Version of the Bible, the word "rekindle" in this verse is translated "fan into flame." This is the idea that when oxygen hits a spark, it can grow into a larger fire. On Pentecost, when the Holy Spirit first came to live in believers permanently, He is described as coming down like tongues of fire and with the sound of a violent wind (see Acts 2:1-4). These two things embody what we need to grow in our spiritual gifts: we need the Spirit Himself, and we need to use the gifts He has given us. This allows Him to fan into flame the spark He has placed in us.

What specific thing can you do to allow the Holy Spirit to "fan into flame" the spiritual gifts He has given you?

The reality is, you may have a spiritual gift that you aren't great at using yet. If this is the case, keep trying. You probably weren't very good the first time you picked up a video game controller or a golf club or a guitar. But you felt drawn to these things, and enjoyed them, so you kept working at it. The same thing can happen with spiritual gifts. It takes time for the Holy Spirit to continue to use you, develop you, and mature you as you exercise your gifts.

> What is a spiritual gift that you have grown in your ability to use over time? How has God grown you in that gift?

Here's the bottom line: keep trying. Don't give up. When an opportunity arises to try something new—like work in the nursery, run sound equipment, lead a Bible study for your team, or be a door greeter—go for it! You don't have to do it forever. Just try long enough to see if this is an area where God can use the gifts He has given you. Remember, God has not given you a spirit of fear, but one of love, power (His power), and sound judgment (see 2 Tim. 1:7).

TWO FINAL THOUGHTS

1. **Can your gifts change?** The Bible is not clear on this, but what is clear is that as you mature and experience things, God can "fan into flame" gifts that might not have been as obvious in your life when you were younger. Keep trying new things and be open to what the Holy Spirit may be wanting to do in and through you.

2. **Seek accountability for using your spiritual gifts.** Remember, you are part of the body of Christ. You may be an ear and not an eye (see 1 Cor. 12:16), but you are incredibly important to the body. Use what you have been given and don't envy what others have.

CLOSE IN PRAYER.

> Thank You, God, for making me gifted. Please fan into flame the gifts that You have given me as I try new things and seek to grow in my ability to use them. Amen.

Read Matthew 25:14-30 in your own Bible.

This is a parable of Jesus about using what He has given you well. It's not about talent in the "things you're good at" sense of the word. The idea of the parable is that whatever He has given you, be faithful with it and use it for His kingdom. This is perfectly applied to spiritual gifts.

> Consider where you might have been gifted by the Holy Spirit. What is one way you can begin to use that gift right now?

This parable isn't implying that if you use your spiritual gifts well, God will give you more spiritual gifts. However, it does mean that when you use whatever God has given you well, He will entrust you with more opportunity to use what He has given you.

> What is an area where God has entrusted you with something (even something other than a spiritual gift) and you can use it well for His kingdom?

Don't bury your gifts. Seek God, ask Him for opportunities to use what He has given you, and use it faithfully.

CLOSE IN PRAYER.

> Lord, thank You for the gifts You have given me. I don't want to bury them. I desire to use them well, for Your kingdom and Your glory. Please give me wisdom as I seek You. Amen.

For we are his workmanship, created in Christ Jesus for good works, which God prepared ahead of time for us to do.

We are God's, and He is working in us to fulfill His plan. No, our good works do not save us, but our good works do reveal whose we are. Desire to use the spiritual gifts God has given you for good works, to show the world that you belong to Jesus, to the glory of God!

Let's memorize this verse as a reminder of the calling God has placed on our lives.

F___ w_ a___ h__ w_____, c_____ i_ C_____ J_____
f___ g_____ w_____, w_____ G___ p_____ a_____ o_
t_____ f___ u__ t__ d___. Ephesians 2:10

Repeat this process until you can fill in the blanks without help. Then try it again without using the first letters as a hint.

____ __ ___ ___ _____, _____ ___ _____
_____ ___ _____ _____, _____ _____ _____
_____ ___ _____ ____ ___ ___ ____. Ephesians 2:10

Once you have the verse memorized, write it on a note card. As you memorize more verses, your stack of note cards will grow. Review them frequently. Memorizing Scripture will help you treasure God's Word in your heart.

CLOSE IN PRAYER.

In this book, you have learned four methods of prayer: PRAY, ACTS, the Lord's Prayer, and praying Scripture. For this day, use the method you found most helpful and spend some time in prayer. Like always, don't rush. Spend time praying that God would use you and the gifts He has given you for His glory and to encourage others.

If you need a reminder, here are those prayer methods again:

PRAY:

Pause
Rejoice
Ask
Yield

ACTS:

Adoration
Confession
Thanksgiving
Supplication

The Lord's Prayer can be found in **Matthew 6:9-13** and **Luke 11:2-4.**

You can pray any Scripture, but the Psalms are typically a very good place to begin.

These methods of prayer are tools you can take with you and use in your daily time with the Lord. Remember, if you are still uncertain about what your spiritual gifts are, pray about it.

CLOSE YOUR TIME OF PRAYER IN YOUR OWN WORDS.

KEEP GOING — Day 4

Spend time today silently reflecting on what you have learned this week, journaling, or doing something that reveals the truth of what God has taught you about the importance of spiritual gifts.

REFLECT: What have you learned about how to use your spiritual gifts well?

JOURNAL: Using a notebook or journal, write about how you can use your spiritual gifts in your church, school, home, or anywhere.

GO AND DO: Have you been ignoring the Holy Spirit's prompting you to do something specific? If so, don't put it off. Be obedient to Him in faith and with confidence. Otherwise, spend some time praying specifically about how you can walk closer in step with the Spirit (see Gal. 5:25).

CLOSE IN PRAYER.

Lord, I am grateful for what You have given me and for what I've learned about spiritual gifts. Help me put these things into practice. Encourage me to say yes to opportunities I have to use my spiritual gifts. Amen.

Group Guide

Thank you for your commitment to students—to loving them well and leading them into deeper relationship with God and others. This book is designed to help students know about spiritual gifts and how to practically begin using them in their lives. Follow these steps as you prepare to lead them through the material.

Pray

Before you meet with your group, spend time in prayer. Ask God to prepare you to lead this study and pray specifically for the students in your group before every session. Ask God to prepare them to approach each session with excitement and a desire to learn to follow Jesus more closely.

Prepare

Don't just wing it with the group sessions; come prepared. Review each session thoroughly before presenting the material to students. Use this group guide to help you lead the content in each session. Consider the age, maturity level, and needs of your group as you present the material.

Encourage & Reach Out

Encourage students in your group to complete each "Keep Going" day following the session. These days expand on the subject of each session and broaden students' understanding. Throughout the week, follow up with group members. Consider reaching out about a specific prayer request or diving further into a question a student may have been afraid to ask in front of the whole group.

Evaluate & Adapt

After each session, think about what went well and what might need to change for you to effectively lead the group. Encourage students to keep going and growing as they follow Jesus.

Session 1: Who is the Holy Spirit?

Let's Begin–Icebreaker Option: Give students two minutes to line up in order of age from oldest to youngest. However, do not let them speak, write, or use phones. They can use hand gestures to indicate how old they are. After the two minutes is up, direct them to give their ages to see if they succeeded.

Transition: Truthfully, no one in your group is very old, but there are plenty of older people in the world. According to a study, in 2021, there were nearly 90,000 people over 100 years old in the United States alone![1]

The One with No Beginning

Students may know that the Holy Spirit has been around a long time, but it's important they also know that He wasn't created—He has always been. Today we're going to talk about who the Holy Spirit is and how He operates in our lives.

Key Scripture: Genesis 1:1-2

Key Question:
Why is it important that God the Father, God the Son (Jesus), and God the Holy Spirit all worked together in the creation of the world and everything that exists?

The Role of the Holy Spirit

The work of the Holy Spirit is different from the work of God the Father, and it's different than the work of God the Son, Jesus.

Key Scripture: John 16:7-15

The Holy Spirit is our Counselor. He convicts us, and He guides us in truth.

Key Questions:
Who has been a good counselor to you? What makes someone a good counselor?

What does it feel like when the Holy Spirit convicts you?

When has the Holy Spirit guided you in the truth, changing your mind from a wrongly held belief to a right one?

The Holy Spirit Lives Within Us

Jesus died, rose again, and ascended to heaven. Now the Holy Spirit lives in those who have placed their faith in Jesus.

Key Scripture: Acts 2:1-4

On the day of Pentecost, the Holy Spirit came to live in the lives of believers forever, and He gave gifts to them to use for glorifying God and building up the church. He still does these two things today.

Key Questions:
What are some signs that the Holy Spirit lives within someone?

How does it make you feel to know that the Holy Spirit has gifted you to serve God?

Close in prayer.
Remember to record prayer requests and to follow up. Encourage students to complete their four "Keep Going" days before the next group meeting.

Session 2: Why Are Spiritual Gifts Important?

Let's Begin—Icebreaker Option: Direct students to create a human knot by standing shoulder to shoulder. Instruct them to reach their right hands into the center of the circle and grab hands with another student (other than the students standing next to them). Then have them repeat this with their left hands. Give them three minutes to untangle the human knot without letting go of each others' hands (it's normal for some students to be facing inside the circle at the end and others to be facing outside the circle).

Transition: Point out that when students formed the knot, they were like one giant body, but it took all of them working together to twist and untangle to form the circle.

One Body, Many Parts

Key Scripture: Romans 12:4-5

Each follower of Jesus is like a different part of the body. All are important. Every person has a role to play in the body of Christ.

Key Question:

Think about the church you are a part of. How have you seen people with different gifts serve in different ways?

Good Stewards

God calls us to use the gifts that He has given us well.

Key Scripture: 1 Peter 4:10-11

Key Points and Questions:

When have you agreed to be a good steward of something that belonged to someone else?

List three ways we steward our spiritual gifts well according to 1 Peter 4:10-11.

The gifts God has given us are intended to be used for His glory and to build up the church, not for our own fame.

Six Important Elements about Spiritual Gifts

1. Spiritual gifts help us understand God.
2. Spiritual gifts help us understand ourselves.
3. Spiritual gifts help us understand the church.
4. Spiritual gifts equip us to fulfill God's mission.
5. Spiritual gifts equip us to serve the body of Christ.
6. Spiritual gifts help us display Jesus in our lives.

Close in prayer.

Remember to record prayer requests and to follow up. Encourage students to complete their four personal study days before the next group meeting.

Session 3: What are the Spiritual Gifts?

Let's Begin—Icebreaker Option: As students arrive, place a sticky note on their heads so no one can see his or her own note. On half of the notes, write the name of a superhero (such as Superman, Spider-Man, or Captain Marvel). On the other half of the notes, write those heroes' alter egos (for the heroes listed, this would be Clark Kent, Peter Parker or Miles Morales, and Carol Danvers). Direct students to ask each other questions to figure out who their heroes are and find their matches.

Transition: These superheroes have special powers that have caused them to use secret identities. As believers with spiritual gifts, our "powers" are from the Holy Spirit and are an important part of our identities as followers of Jesus.

Two Types of Gifts

Key Scripture: 1 Peter 4:11

There are two broad categories of spiritual gifts: **serving gifts** and **speaking gifts**.

Serving Gifts: Administration, Leadership, Helps and Service, Mercy, Giving, Faith, Healing, and Miracles.

Serving gifts are described as "people focused." People with serving gifts are often those who can make things happen.

Key Question

Of the serving gifts we've just discussed, which ones have made the biggest impact on your life? How have you been impacted by them?

Speaking Gifts: Apostleship, Evangelism, Prophecy, Teaching, Exhortation, Discernment, Tongues, and the Interpretation of tongues.

Speaking the words of God is a holy calling and never to be done lightly or for selfish gain.

Key Question
Who has taught you from the Bible or encouraged you in a way that helped you and shaped your life? How did this person do this?

Close in prayer.
Remember to record prayer requests and follow up. Encourage students to complete their four "Keep Going" days before the next group meeting.

Session 4: How do I Learn What My Spiritual Gifts Are?

Let's Begin—Icebreaker Option: Bring three identically wrapped presents to your group meeting. In one, have a nice gift, like a $10 gift card. In another, have something like a full-sized candy bar. In the final box, have something small, like a peppermint or a single piece of hard candy. Determine three winners from the group (in any way you choose, such as a game of Rock, Paper, Scissors, or by putting sticky notes under three chairs before the group meets) and call them up. Let them pick out which gifts they want. Give them a chance to trade if they want, then let them unwrap their gifts.

Transition: Sometimes when we get a gift, it can be a bit of a letdown. But it's never disappointing when we discover our spiritual gifts and use them to serve God's kingdom.

Who Are You?

Key Scripture: Psalm 139:1-16

God knows you, designed you, and gave you the gifts He intended for you to have.

Key Questions
What are you good at? What talents, skills, and abilities do you have?

What things are you interested in or passionate about?

Ask a friend or leader in your church to answer the same two questions about you.

It's important to remember that talents, abilities, interests, passions, and spiritual gifts are not always the same.

What does the Bible Say?

1. Each believer was given at least one spiritual gift the moment the Holy Spirit came to live in him or her.
2. All the gifts are given to glorify God and for building up the church.
3. All the gifts are important, even though they have different functions and purposes within the church.
4. All the gifts are to be used humbly and through the power God provides, not for selfish gain.

Key Questions

Of the spiritual gifts listed in this book (see pages 75-76) which ones stand out to you as possibilities for the gift(s) you have been given?

Ask a friend or church leader if she or he has noticed something special about you that you might not have noticed about yourself.

What Do I Do Now?

Key Scripture: Mark 10:43-45

The path to greatness in Jesus's kingdom is through service. Start out with the desire to serve Him through your spiritual gifts and you will be starting out on the right foot.

Key Question

What are ways you can serve Jesus right now in your church, school, home, or neighborhood?

1. Ask God to help you know your gifts.
2. Ask God to give you opportunities to try things.
3. Listen for the Holy Spirit affirming your gifts through others.

Close in prayer.

Remember to record prayer requests and follow up. Encourage students to complete their four "Keep Going" days before the next group meeting.

Session 5: How Do I Use My Spiritual Gifts?

Let's Begin—Icebreaker Option: As students enter the room, give each of them a strip of paper and a pencil or pen. Instruct students to write any question they may still have about spiritual gifts on their strips of paper. Gather the slips of paper to read and provide answers (if you can) as you work through the rest of today's session. Hopefully the content from rest of the session will help answer some of their remaining questions. ***Note**: It's okay if you don't know the answer to a question. The worst thing to do is to make up an answer to avoid looking like you don't have all the answers.*

Transition: Tell students that for the rest of the session, you'll try to answer some of the questions they might still have about spiritual gifts.

Key Scripture: 1 Timothy 4:14-15

Talents and Spiritual Gifts

Talents and spiritual gifts are not always the same thing, but spiritual gifts can enhance and come alongside talents.

Key Questions
What are some talents that aren't spiritual gifts?

How can you use a talent like basketball or playing the trumpet alongside a spiritual gift?

How could a talent complement the following three spiritual gifts? Helps and Service; Administration; Teaching

Where Can You Use Spiritual Gifts?

You do not have to use spiritual gifts only within the walls of a church building.

Key Questions
How can you use spiritual gifts at home? At school? In your neighborhood? On the internet?

Spiritual gifts are intended to be used in community.

Fan Into Flame

Key Scripture: 2 Timothy 1:6-7

To grow in our spiritual gifts, we must use them, even if we're not great to begin with.

Key Questions

What is a spiritual gift that you have grown in your ability to use over time? How has God grown you in that gift?

Two Final Thoughts

1. **Can your gifts change?** The Bible is not clear, but keep trying new things and be open to what the Holy Spirit may be wanting to do in and through you.
2. **Seek accountability for using your spiritual gifts.**

Close in prayer.

SPIRITUAL GIFTS LIST

Administration: People who have this gift can organize and mobilize others in ways that are vital for a healthy church community (see 1 Cor. 12:28).

Apostleship: The gift of apostleship today is connected to missions and a desire and supernatural ability to help the gospel spread to places where it is not (see 1 Cor. 12:28; Eph. 4:11).

Discernment: Those with the gift of discernment know what is true and what is untrue and lovingly help others know the difference as well (see 1 Cor. 12:10).

Evangelism: Those with the gift of evangelism—sharing the gospel with others—can build relationships, process and communicate deep theological truths and help others learn how to effectively share Jesus with people as well (see Eph. 4:11).

Exhortation: The gift of exhortation is a supernatural combination of the abilities to comfort, counsel, and encourage others (see Rom. 12:8).

Faith: Those with the gift of faith have a supernatural trust in God that allows them to move with confidence and assurance when others might not (see Rom. 12:9).

Giving: Those with the gift of giving do so in a selfless way that's empowered by the Holy Spirit. Giving is their first instinct (see Rom. 12:8).

Healing: In the Bible there are many example of healings. This gift is less common today, but that doesn't mean it doesn't happen. The gift of healing is the supernatural ability to restore someone to health. If healing occurs today, it is always in the capacity of service to others, and not in a self-glorifying or self-promoting way (see 1 Cor. 12:9-10).

Helps and Service: People with this gift have been given a supernatural gift of being able to help and willingly serve. This gift is often expressed in a willingness to do practical jobs that others don't want to do (see 1 Cor. 12:28; Rom. 12:7).

Leadership: Those with the gift of leadership have a vision and can articulate it and lead others into the future (see Rom. 12:8).

Mercy: Those with the gift of mercy can show compassion and offer hope in a unique, God-sized way (see Rom. 12:8).

Miracles: Like healing, miracles were crucial in biblical times. Miracles still occur today, but they are clearly less common than in the New Testament. If the miraculous occurs, it is to God's glory and not for the fame and fortune of any individual using the gift (see 1 Cor. 12:9-10).

Prophecy: This gift has two components: foretelling and forth-telling. Yes, sometimes a person is gifted to tell what will happen in the future ("foretelling"). However, today prophecy is more exhibited in the ability to diagnose a situation and share the truth of God's Word with people in impactful ways that speak to their lives and circumstances ("forth-telling") (see Rom. 12:6; 1 Cor. 12:10; Eph. 4:11).

Teaching: The gift of teaching is the ability to explain God's Word to others in a way they can understand it and apply it to their lives (see Rom. 12:7; Eph. 4:11).

Tongues/Interpretation of Tongues: The gift of tongues is the ability to speak in other languages. The gift of interpretation is the ability to communicate what is said in those other languages to those who hear the one speaking in tongues. These are two separate gifts, but when they are used, one must always go with the other (see 1 Cor. 12:10,28,30).

SOURCES

Session 2

1. Richard Marquand, dir., *Return of the Jedi* (1983; Los Angeles, CA: 20th Century Studios), film.

Session 3

1. For example: Ron Dante, *The Amazing Spider-Man: From Beyond The Grave: A Rockomic,* recorded 1972, Buddah Records, vinyl LP; Mary Wolfman and Stan Lee, *The Amazing Spider-Man*, no. 20 (Marvel Comics: 1980); Sam Raimi, dir., *Spider-Man* (Culvert City, CA: Columbia, 2002).

2. Dan Darling, *Spiritual Gifts: What They Are and How to Use Them* (Brentwood, TN: Lifeway Christian Resources, 2022), 29.

3. Darling, *Spiritual Gifts*, 30.

4. Darling, *Spiritual Gifts*, 30.

5. Darling, *Spiritual Gifts*, 43.

Group Guide

1. Thomas Peris, "Centenarian Statistics," Chobanian & Avedisian School of Medicine, accessed December 7, 2023, https://www.bumc.bu.edu/centenarian/statistics/

NOTES

Get the most out of this book.

Customize your Bible study time with a guided experience and additional resources.

ADDITIONAL RESOURCES

Gifted (eBook)
A five-session study on spiritual gifts.
Visit lifeway.com/gifted

Follower
An eight-week study for new believers in Christ.
Visit lifeway.com/follower

Lifeway Students Devotions
Help students begin the habit of daily time in the Word through Lifeway Students Devotions.
Visit lifeway.com/teendevotionals

Too many believers feel that to serve in the church, you have to be part of some elite team of super-Christians. This couldn't be further from the truth. The reality is, if you've placed your faith in Jesus, you have been given gifts that are designed to be used to serve God. Every believer is gifted. The question is, how has the Holy Spirit gifted you? And how can you put your gifts to work for God's kingdom? This book will help you find answers to these questions and more!

Each chapter contains in depth exploration of spiritual gifts and truths that students need to grasp as they grow in their faith. Topics include:

Who is the Holy Spirit?

Why are spiritual gifts important?

What are the spiritual gifts?

What are my spiritual gifts?

How do I use my spiritual gifts?

This book can be used with both individuals and groups.

Lifeway designs trustworthy experiences that fuel ministry. Today, the ministries of Lifeway reach more than 160 countries around the globe. For specific information on Lifeway Students, visit lifeway.com/students.

 For more resources scan the QR code or go to lifeway.com/gifted.